THE NARWHAL

Do Your Kids Know This?

A Children's Picture Book
Amazing Creature Series

Tanya Turner

PUBLISHED BY:

Tanya Turner

TABLE OF CONTENTS

The Narwhal

The Narwhal.
Image from Shutterstock by Andreas Meyer.

The Narwhal is also called Narwhale – and rightfully so, as it is indeed a species of whale. It's a medium-sized whale, to be more specific.

What makes this sea creature unique and extra special is that it has a really long tusk that makes it entirely different from other species of whales (and other sea animals, for that matter). Also, its tusk, which is similar to an elephant's tusk, is actually a tooth. Have you ever seen a tooth as big (and as long)?

Needless to say, this creature's tusk is its main attraction. Some people see it as a sword – although that's not an accurate description with regards to its use since the Narwhal really doesn't use its tusk as a weapon.

There is something really special about the shape and overall structure of the Narwhal's tusk though. Their tusks were actually worth a lot of money in the past because they were sold as

Unicorn's horns. Since a Unicorn is a magical creature, their horns are thought of as magical and lucky.

Moreover, because of their Unicorn-like tusk, Narwhals are also called Unicorns of the Sea – even to this very day.

Have you seen a Narwhal?

Would you like to meet it?

You can get to know it better and see it up close through the pages of this book.

Getting to Know the Narwhal

Being a medium-sized species of whale, the Narwhal can have a body length of 13 to 18 feet. Note, however, that the males are larger than the females. As adults, they can weigh anywhere from

1,800 to 3,500 pounds. This is a normal weight for whales and other sea creatures because they are big animals.

The Narwhal's head (especially the forehead part) is rounded – and this makes their appearance unique from other types of whales (except for Beluga whales, which also have rounded foreheads). Also, like Beluga whales, they also have short snouts. Actually, the Narwhal's shape is very similar to the Beluga whale's shape. Their identifying mark, however, is their long tusks.

Their tusks are actually teeth, but each Narwhal usually has just one tooth that grows really long. It's always their left tooth located in their upper jaws – and this one tooth punctures the sea creature's lip as it develops into a tusk.

As previously said, only one tooth per Narwhal develops into a tusk. However, though very rarely, a Narwhal can have 2 tusks.

But again, this seldom happens – only one out of 500 Narwhals

has two tusks.

Views from the side and under the Narwhal.

Image from Wikimedia by W. Scoresby.

Only male Narwhals have these tusks. Some females can have

them too, but this is very rare. In fact, only about 15 percent of female Narwhals usually have tusks. If the females do develop tusks, they are smaller and less elaborate. The male Narwhals' tusks have spiral markings on them. In the females, these markings are usually absent.

What's really amazing about their tusks is that they can grow really long. The reason for this is that their tusks continue to grow throughout their entire lives. Old Narwhals can have tusks anywhere from 4 feet 11 inches to 10 feet and 2 inches long, which is a really long tusk!

Because of the size of their tusk, you can expect this type of tooth to be around 22 pounds for an adult Narwhal. For a creature that weighs over a thousand pounds, that's quite normal.

Remember that the tusk continues to grow throughout the Narwhal's life, so it is not a dead structure, but actually has nerves and feelings that make it a "live" part of their body.

Think about your own teeth for a second. However, the structure of Narwhal's teeth is different – quite the opposite of the human teeth, actually.

Try tapping on your teeth, for example, and you won't feel any pain. That's because the outside portion of your teeth is not very sensitive, but the inside portion of your teeth are sensitive because that's where the nerves are.

In the case of the Narwhals, their tusks are hollow inside and the nerve endings are located outside. Therefore, their tusks are very sensitive to the touch. In fact, around 10 million nerve endings make up the outside portion of their tusks.

The Narwhal's tusk also serves as its sensory organ because of its sensitivity, so the whale uses it as it goes about its life in the sea. Its tusk helps the Narwhal explore its environment and sense danger.

The Narwhal's color also sets it apart from other sea creatures. It has blackish and brownish patterns over its white body. They are in their darkest shade while still young, but their overall color will fade into white as they grow older. You can even recognize the really old individuals through their color because they can be all white when they reach a really old age.

A Narwhal underwater.

Habitat

The population of Narwhals can be found in the Arctic waters along Canada, Greenland, and Russia.

They usually stay near the surface of the water, but can dive really deep and stay underwater for a long time.

Behavior

Narwhals are social animals and usually stay in groups of five or more individuals (sometimes around 20). In some cases, the groups are made up of females and their young ones (their offspring). There are also times when mixed groups of males, females and young make up a group. During the summer months, however, the groups can expand as different groups join together in one big group. When this happens, a really large group made up of 500 to 1,000 individuals can form a group.

As social creatures, Narwhals also communicate with one another – and there are a lot of ways for them to do this. Clicking their tongues is a common communication technique among whales. They can engage in whistling like dolphins (they are related to dolphins, by the way), and they can also produce knocking sounds through their blow holes.

Narwhals have blow holes like other types of whales. Remember, they are mammals and are air-breathing creatures. They use their blow holes to release used up air before inhaling fresh air again.

Although they mostly stay near the surface of the water (and you will see their tusks on the surface of the water) they are also capable of diving really deep – as deep as 4,900 feet. They hold their breath when they are underwater and can usually stay there for about 25 mins.

A group of Narwhals.

Image from Shutterstock by Linda Bucklin.

Keep in mind that Narwhals can drown – because they can't breathe under the water They really can't stay very long underwater because they need to come to the surface to breathe.

When in deep water, Narwhals use echolocation to find their way. This is an effective method for avoiding obstacles and for finding prey or live food to eat. Echolocation is also useful for avoiding predators that may attack and eat them. Echolocation is a method where the Narwhals give off sounds under the water and wait for the sound waves to bounce back at them. They are sensitive to the sound waves and they will know if there are obstacles or animals present within their immediate environment.

Their very sensitive tusks help them sense the things that are around them, too. That's why noise pollution that comes from human construction and shipping activities can be very disturbing for them. It's like being bombarded with irritating noise – which can be very stressful for these whales.

If it were not for noise pollution, their underwater sensitivity would be really helpful to the Narwhals. Their sensitive senses make it easy for them to communicate with one another and to find their way in the seas as well. They also use their senses to find food and mates and to care for their young.

Needless to say, the problem of noise pollution also affects their effectiveness in escaping their predators. Since their senses are disturbed by mixed sound waves, they will find it hard to interpret the things that surround them – and their enemies can get close to them this way.

A preserved tusk of the Narwhal.

Image from Flickr by Brian Suda.

Narwhals are slow swimmers. Because of this, their chances of escaping their predators using speed can be useless. Their enemies will almost always catch up with them and kill them, so the best way for the Narwhals to escape their enemies is to hide.

You might think that it's very difficult for the Narwhal to hide itself since it's quite a big sea creature – and you're right. However, keep in mind that there are rocks, plants and caves under the sea that can be used as hiding places. The Narwhals use such places to escape from possible attacks.

Another interesting behavior of the Narwhal is called "tusking." With this activity, you will see the Narwhals rubbing their tusks with one another. It is not fighting when you see them doing this – they are simply exchanging information through the water chemistry present on their tusks.

Diet

Narwhals suck in their prey with their mouths. They usually feed on small sea creatures like fish, crabs, shrimps, squids, etc.

Reproduction

Male Narwhals become fully mature at 11 to 13 years old, where they are around 12 feet 10 inches long. The females, on the other hand, mature at about five to eight years old – and they will be around 11 feet 2 inches at this point in their lives. As mature Narwhals, they can start breeding when it's mating season.

It will take about 14 months for a pregnant Narwhal to give birth. A mother Narwhal will usually give birth to just one offspring which can be about 5.2 feet long. A newly born Narwhal can weigh about 175 to 220 pounds – which is the weight of a big adult person. Its color as a young Narwhal will be dark gray.

Because it is a mammal, the young Narwhal will be fed with milk from its mother. It will stay with its mother (while feeding on milk) for about 20 months. During all this time, its mother will teach its young survival skills in the water.

A mature female Narwhal can give birth to an offspring every three years. This gives her enough time to properly care for her young and ensure its survival.

Narwhals are also called Unicorns of the Sea.

Image from Shutterstock by Michael Vigliotti.

Status

The population of Narwhals is still quite high, so they are not considered an endangered species at this point in time. However, they currently are labeled with the Near Threatened status, which means that their population could be in danger any time soon – unless conservation efforts are taken as soon as possible.

Conservation

Because of their Near Threatened status, countries are now banning the importation of Narwhal tusks. Taking a tusk from a Narwhal will kill the animal.

In places where it's legal to catch Narwhals as sources of food and clothing, a limit on the number of allowable catches is also in place.

Threats

While Narwhals have a lot of predators and enemies under the sea, other factors threaten their survival. Noise pollution and climate change are just two of the things that affect their health and shorten their lives.

People are also considered to be their biggest threat. Almost all parts of the Narwhals are usable to humans. Their meat can be eaten, their skin can be used for clothing materials, their organs can be used as sources for oil, and so on and so forth, and you already know that their tusks are in high demand.

Life Span

Narwhals have long lives and can live up to 50 years. However, many of them don't get to reach such an old age because they

A beautiful Narwhal.

Image from Shutterstock by Andreas Meyer.

usually die of suffocation under the water. Remember, they live in

Arctic waters – which has ice. They can get trapped when the

surface of the water freezes or they can get trapped among ice

formations when traveling to the open seas.

Love for Narwhals

Narwhals are amazing and lovable creatures. They are as magical as mythical unicorns – except that they're real.

As one of the rarest animals in the world, not too many people know about them. Show them your love by sharing what you know about them with your friends.

Made in the USA
Middletown, DE
20 August 2019